Cuauhtémoc Cárdenas

and the Roots of Mexico's New Democracy

By Robert Richter

John Gordon Burke Publisher, Inc.

Contemporary Profiles and Policy Series for the Younger Reader

Library of Congress Cataloging-in-Publication Data

Richter, Robert, 1948–
    Cuauhtémoc Cárdenas and the roots of Mexico's new democracy / by Robert Richter.
        p. cm. — (Contemporary profiles and policy series for the younger reader)
        Includes bibliographical references and index.
        ISBN 0–934272–66–2 (alk. paper). — ISBN 0–934272–65–4 (pbk. : alk. paper)

    1. Cârdenas Solârzano, Cuauhtâmoc—Juvenile literature. 2. Mexico– Politics and Government–1988–Juvenile literature. 3. Governors–Mexico– Michoacân de Ocampo (Mexico)–Biography–Juvenile literature 4. Mayors– Mexico–Mexico City–Biography–Juvenile literature 5. Presidential candidates– Mexico–Biography–Juvenile literature [1. Cârdenas Solârzano, Cuauhtâmoc. 2. Presidential candidates–Mexico. 3. Mexico–Politics and government– 1988–.] I. Title. II. Series.
F1236.6.C37 C84 2001
972'.530836'092–dc21
[B]   00–045545

Credits: Cover Design: Tissi Blount/M&H Design; Front cover photograph: Mariana Yampolsky; Photographs Back cover and Page 4: Mayo-Borzelli/Integra Servicios.
Copyright©2000 by John Gordon Burke Publisher, Inc.
Printed and Bound in the United States of America

TABLE OF CONTENTS

Cuauhtémoc Cárdenas Solórzano

Mayo-Borzelli /Integra Servicios

CHAPTER I: The Presidential Election, 1988

Early in 1988, the campaign for the presidency of Mexico was sizing up to be like all the previous ones before it. Since 1928 Mexico's president has been elected to a six-year term, and he is constitutionally prohibited from seeking reelection. However, while in office, the president commands absolute authority over all aspects of government and economy in Mexico. Traditionally, one of the final and most important decisions the president of Mexico makes is choosing his successor. In 1987 Miguel de la Madrid was finishing out his term in office when he made his *destape*—literally, his *revelation*—that Carlos Salinas de Gotari would be his party's next candidate for president.

Although Carlos Salinas had yet to campaign and be formally elected by democratic vote, all of Mexico knew that Salinas would be the next president, no matter who ran against him. While Mexico is considered a democracy, and its people vote for candidates for office, there is only one major political party. That party, called the Partido Revolucionario Institucional (Institutional Revolutionary Party), or PRI, is virtually indistinguishable from the government itself. Since its founding in 1929, and up until the 1988 races, PRI had won every major election in every national, state, and municipal race for office in every year. But in the late 1980s, something was changing in Mexico.

Mexico's one-party system had created a political stability through six decades that allowed Mexico to become the most peaceful and advanced Latin American country of the twentieth century. But with continuous rule by a single, powerful group in a government, there is no system of checks and balances. With no congressional forum where equally powerful groups can maintain a watchdog criticism of the ruling party, there is an open invitation to fraud, corruption, and self-enrichment, using inside knowledge and preferential treatment for business friends. In 1988 Mexico was a modern nation, but also a nation of great contrast between a few rich and many poor citizens. Those in the upper echelons of government and PRI party politics were also those who controlled virtually all of the press, industry, business and labor interests of the nation.

Government leaders could award rich building contracts to members of their own families who owned the industries that could do the work. Newspapers and broadcast journalists were on government payrolls. Office holders could give jobs and contracts to family and favored friends. This type of government has been called the Spoils System, and even early U.S. government suffered somewhat from the problem, but the two-party system of democracy has helped contain and control that problem. This has not been the case in Mexico.

By the mid-1980s, fraud and corruption for personal gain was rampant in Mexican government and business. Fewer and fewer within PRI were getting richer, while most Mexicans suffered from a depressed economy and the lifestyle of a Third World nation. Going into the 1988 election, the situation was apparent to most Mexicans, but what could they do about it? The PRI held power, and elections were an empty formality. President De la Madrid had pointed the *dedazo*—literally, the big finger—at Carlos Salinas. Salinas would be "elected" supreme leader, President of Mexico, and life would go on like always.

Unless a miracle occurred. Unless a unique opposition candidate would emerge from the shadow of PRI to speak for the common Mexican and change the course of national history. It had to be someone almost unimaginable; someone knowledgeable in the ways and means of political power, but more interested in the welfare of his fellow countryman than in personal wealth; someone with a name and image that merited respect and trust; someone with proven integrity and experience who could launch a renegade candidacy that would not be dismissed as foolish or hopeless, or motivated by desire for personal power. It had to be someone who could speak for common people and advocate a more fair, more open democracy; call for government by more people; call for an economy that benefited the entire nation and not just a few.

What the poor and disenfranchised people of Mexico

needed was a biblical David to face the giant Goliath of PRI, an underdog to stand up to the bully. They needed someone to unite the vote of millions of discontented, cynical, and powerless people; win the reins of government; and change the course of Mexico's history.

Early in 1988, the miracle began to happen. An unexpected hero stepped forward. Perhaps it seemed sudden, but he had always been there, generally ignored and despised—or used, by those in power. His independent candidacy was supported timidly at first by small radical groups, but his message was heard by the dispossessed and underprivileged. His family background and personal character helped rally support. By the July election, an undeniable groundswell of enthusiasm and hope placed this man in a position to actually challenge the ruling party's 60-year strangle hold on the powers of government. This man was Cuauhtémoc Cárdenas de Solórzano.

On the surface, Cuauhtémoc Cárdenas seemed an unlikely person to become the people's opposition candidate. He was the son of Mexico's most honored and respected past president, Lázaro Cárdenas, who actually helped found the PRI. Beside Lázaro Cárdenas, few had done as much to see governing power consolidated in the hands of just one man (the president) and his closest advisors. Cuauhtémoc grew up in Mexico's presidential home and has personally known all the country's presidents since his own father picked his own successor in 1940 and relinquished power. His son, Cuauhtémoc, attended private schools and the Autonomous National University of Mexico (UNAM–Universidad Nacional Autonomía de Mexico) to become a civil engineer.

Cárdenas worked in Mexico's steel industry, in dam construction, and on irrigation projects. He took directorships and administrative positions by presidential appointment. In 1980, with little political experience, he was hand-picked by then-President López Portillo to be PRI candidate (and therefore, assured election) for the governorship of his home state of Michoacán. Cuauhtémoc Cárdenas could have been considered an ultimate "insider" with the ruling establishment, in position to take advantage of "business as usual" in Mexico in the 1980s.

But those in the party elite, who expected Cárdenas to be like them, didn't realize the power of his father's personal influence on Cuauhtémoc's life and perceptions. Lázaro Cárdenas' idealistic belief in justice and honesty, and his true compassion for the disadvantaged had also become the hallmarks of his son's political philosophy. By the end of his term as governor of Michoacán in 1986, Cuauhtémoc Cárdenas was having serious doubts about PRI's commitment to helping the poor, and to the just observance of constitutional laws. He simply wanted the government's actions to match their promises to the people, but he didn't see this happening.

Cárdenas began to make his objections to party rule known publicly, and he angered PRI party leaders who had no intention of sharing power with other interests. Despite warnings, Cárdenas and a few supporters pressed for liberalizing the Institutional Revolutionary Party, wanting to abandon the *destape,*the presidential anointing of a successor, giving rank and file party members the chance to elect a candidate. Though reprimanded, Cárdenas helped form The Democratic Current, a formal faction within the PRI that clamored for democratic change. In 1987, PRI leadership responded by expelling these "rebels" from the party. Cárdenas was then nominated as a presidential candidate by The Authentic Party of the Mexican Revolution (PARM–Partido Auténtico Revolucionario Mexicano), and the stage was set for the July 1988 election.

There had always been other small political parties in Mexico, but they traditionally represented minor radical groups with narrow and hard-line political perspectives. There were communist and socialist parties, anti-communist Catholic activists, and conservative free trade advocates. In 1939, the National Action Party (PAN–Partido Accíon Nacional) had been created and represented mostly small businessmen and conservative persons who were Catholics and who favored personal rights over the state's economic control. In all previous elections, small parties put up candidates against the PRI political machine, but numbers and wealth, media and ballot box control always favored the PRI. Small parties, that argued amongst themselves and split the opposition vote, gave the PRI its disguise of legitimate democracy and fair elections. Except for a few minor positions in congress, these parties never won office.

In early 1988 Cárdenas's campaign seemed to be just another version of this pattern, but slowly, a political miracle began to occur. Lacking every advantage the PRI candidate, Carlos Salinas, had—money, armies of advisors, influence peddlers, and media control—Cárdenas had begun an eight-month campaign by flying from town to town in a small plane, landing to speak to small groups of workers and peasants and shop owners. He accepted the support of other small parties and splinter groups with little prestige or influence and few followers.

Tirelessly, Cárdenas argued that government economic policy favored only the rich Mexican capitalist, not the average man in the street who slaved in a depressed economy. He argued against the mass privatization of business and industry, especially by foreign interests. He spoke out for more choice by common people in the affairs of national government. Underscored by a poor standard of living and by government promises that never came true, his simple, honest message touched a collective nerve of hope in many Mexicans. They began to believe in the possibilities Cárdenas represented.

In February, 1988, when Cárdenas returned to the La Laguna region of Michoacán, he found thousands of supporters in the streets. There were no slick campaign events and displays—no money for that. There were simply people, a few homemade signs, and children with their welcome banners. People were remembering the achievements of his father and seeing in this son a new representative of earlier, responsive government.

Crowds began to multiply in other places, too: in Baja California, Vera Cruz, and in Mexico City where 100,000 students, professors, workers, and store owners welcomed him respectfully. Other small political parties that at first had doubted Cárdenas' sincere break from the powerful PRI offered their official support. Yet just a week before the July election, he still had no unified party behind him, just the wide-ranging support of peasants, students, workers, professionals, feminists, ecologists, old nationalists, ex-PRI members, and just about everybody else who ever felt their vote had never meant anything before this election. A collective enthusiasm swept over Mexico. "Cárdenas for President" was the talk in cafes and work places, over family dinners, in buses and stores. He had awakened a new will to power through political participation in millions who felt they had no place in the PRI monopoly over economy and government. A new feeling arose that there was finally a chance to challenge—and even to beat—the establishment power, in the Mexican senate and municipal races, and even in the presidency itself. Millions turned out on election day for Cárdenas.

Yet despite the new hope and votes Cárdenas generated in the Mexican people, PRI candidate Salinas de Gotari declared victory. In a matter of days, it became clear that the election had been fraudulently stolen by the powerful political machinery of the PRI. There were protests in the streets in cities all over Mexico for weeks after. Finally, a few positions in senate, gubernatorial, and municipal offices were conceded to opposition candidates, but the PRI kept its grip on the governing machinery of Mexico.

Yet the presidential election of 1988 had repercussions that are echoing through Mexican politics and government into the 21st century. Great change is taking place, and Cuauhtémoc Cárdenas has been its instrumental force. He will affect Mexican government and history for years to come and may yet be the nation's leader.

Who is this man who has brought new optimism to average Mexican voters? What have they seen in him that inspired their confidence, trust, and new hope? How has he managed what no one else has since 1938: to infuse the common people with a new sense of national pride and power? Who is Cuauhtémoc Cárdenas?

CHAPTER II: Modern Mexico and Lázaro Cárdenas

To understand the significance of the 1988 presidential election and Mexico's new democratic trends, it's necessary to know something about Mexico's history since its revolution (1910-1920) against the dictatorship of Porfirio Díaz. The significance of Cuauhtémoc Cárdenas' role in 1988, and in the future of Mexico's politics, can be found in his personal family history. Cuauhtémoc's life has been linked to Mexican political history since before his birth.

Once the Díaz dictatorship was overthrown, the Mexican Revolution became a violent class struggle between regional armies. A constitution had been created in 1917, but disagreements of interpretation and enforcement of laws always deteriorated into armed conflict between regional "caudillos," or military men with personal armies. Until 1928 every elected or appointed Mexican ruler met a violent end at the hands of opponents when political fortunes shifted. Ex-president Álvaro Obregón was assassinated in 1928, in part, because he sought reelection, which is anti-constitutional in Mexico.

General Elías Calles was then president (1924-1928), and he called for a congress of all military leaders, industrial giants, labor union representatives, large land owners, and political bosses in Mexico to determine together the country's fate. They would rule by consensus, rather than by the decrees of the strongest caudillo. All rival factions would come together to choose a leader, a civilian. This decision-by-committee eventually evolved into the Institutional Revolutionary Party, or PRI. Calles and his handpicked successor, Portes Gil, successfully included every important political group in the country, but Calles was still the real power behind the presidency, and he chose men from this new party whom he could control.

In 1933 Calles picked Lázaro Cárdenas to be president for the first ever six-year term. Cárdenas had served Calles well in the past, first as a subordinate officer during the revolution, and later in official government positions. Lázaro Cárdenas was also shrewd, intelligent, and likable. A political opponent once called him a fox.

At age 18, Lázaro had been thrust into the revolution as a general's secretary because he could read and write. Ten years later he would be the youngest general in Mexico's military. During the violent political chaos of those years, he loyally served under both Calles and Obregón, gaining a reputation for honesty, fairness, compassion for his enemies, and hard work. On two occasions when his troops were defeated by rival factions, Cárdenas was hospitalized and then released by opposing generals because of his honorable reputation and his refusal to take part in bloodthirsty revenge or betrayal. Later, Cárdenas returned the favor, helping a defeated rebel general to reach exile in the United States, angering Obregón, who called him "correct, but incompetent" as a military man.

Another he helped to temporary exile was Francisco Múgica, an author of key articles of the 1917 constitution and governor of Michoacán when President Obregón ordered Lázaro Cárdenas to arrest him. Múgica carried out land reforms that Obregón had halted. Obregón "suggested" that Múgica be shot "while trying to escape." Besides being an honest and fair state governor, Múgica was also an old friend of the Cárdenas family, and the bonds of friendship, honesty, and loyalty in Lázaro easily overrode his sense of duty to extreme orders of violence.

During the Calles presidency, and back in favor, Francisco Múgica became Lázaro's mentor in politics while Lázaro was Chief of Military Operations (1925-28). Múgica had angered President Obregón by distributing thousands of acres of land to hundreds of homeless peasants in Michoacán, just as the constitution actually called for. He also encouraged workers to form unions to fight for rights, and he was very anti-clerical because he felt that the Catholic Church had always helped the rich and powerful to maintain a class system that oppressed and exploited the poor. Múgica introduced Lázaro to these ideas and to their relationship to Karl Marx and communism. Múgica taught that socialism, a nonviolent form of communism, could be an appropriate doctrine for conflict resolution in Mexico, and it was a lesson that Lázaro Cárdenas took to heart and understood.

During the first two decades of the twentieth century, most of western civilization was in violent reaction to the economic consequences of the Industrial Revolution. Owners of industry, natural resources, and business enjoyed prosperity, while factory workers, peasants, and laborers slaved and lived in terrible conditions. As well as the Mexican Revolution, the Bolshevik Revolution overwhelmed Russia, and Europe was engulfed in World War I (1914-1918). Then the Depression of the 1920s hit the U.S. and Europe. People everywhere searched for answers to the economic injustice of the capitalist system in the emerging theories of socialism and communism. Created in those turbulent times, the Constitution of 1917, a troublesome blend of capitalist and socialist principles, was Mexico's response to the nation's chaos.

As governor of Michoacán, Múgica had briefly tried to carry out socialist articles of the constitution. When Lázaro Cárdenas was picked by Calles to be governor of Michoacán in 1928, Lázaro would do the same.

Lázaro was barely 32 when he became governor, and he had had men under his command since he was sixteen. He had developed a natural compassion for Mexico's peasants, particularly the Indians with little or no power or ability to better their personal circumstances. He was also an idealist, and with Múgica's guidance, he also had a clear plan of how to help his fellow countrymen. Within the first year of office, he began to divide the giant, single-family estates, called haciendas, into hundreds of smaller tracts to be managed and farmed by local peasants. These tracts were called *ejidos*. The land was considered property of the state to be allotted to individuals by local *ejido* committees. In four years Cárdenas personally allotted over a quarter of a million acres to nearly 200 villages, more than twice the area all previous governors combined had distributed.

Cárdenas also believed in the dignity and rights of the common worker. Again following Múgica's articles of the constitution, he encouraged agrarian and labor organization to demand and protect rights and wage negotiation for workers. During his governorship, the first formal unions of waiters, shoe shiners, industrial workers, and teachers were allowed to form into one state union. They tried working together to gain better wages and living conditions for all.

While Lázaro was less anti-Catholic than Calles, and Múgica, and others, he developed an army of young, enthusiastic teachers to go out into the country villages to "de-fanaticize and de-alcoholize" the people. These teachers were to bring a socialist education into the small rural schools. They tried to combat conservative clerical ideas with a new, "scientific view of life."

Lázaro was also the consummate politician. When local conflicts arose between socialists and religious conservatives, or between workers and factory owners, or in land distributions procedures, Cárdenas himself would appear in a village or town to personally hear the people's grievances and to propose fair solutions, acting like a benevolent father instead of like the cruel and greedy caudillos of the past. He was the first—and for the most part, only—top government leader to go out to meet the people face to face in their own villages. Just his presence there symbolized the honest concern for local problems that defined Lázaro Cárdenas as a true leader of the common people of Mexico.

As Cárdenas implemented his socialist programs in Michoacán, he also negotiated the ambiguous politics of President Calles' federal government. Cárdenas became president of the ruling political party, helping to consolidate consensus governing among party leaders. He was Minister of the Interior for a brief term, and later, Minister of War and the Navy. By the time of Calles' *destape* that Lázaro Cárdenas would be the next president of Mexico, Cárdenas was a well-liked, highly respected leader with a wide reputation for upright living, honesty, decency, and for being a true provider for the common Mexican man.

By the time he became president in 1934, not yet 40 years old, Lázaro Cárdenas was a leader of great conviction and independent spirit. Like no other leader before, he had gone out into the country to campaign before the people, announcing his intention to extend his political experiments in Michoacán to all of Mexico. His policies and post-presidential accomplishments would have a far-reaching effect on the national character and history of Mexico. He would eventually be honored as Mexico's most moral and conscientious political leader.

Lázaro's personal demeanor and value systems would also have profound effects on friends and family, particularly his son, Cuauhtémoc, who just happened to be born in the middle of the political campaign, only seven months before his father became President of Mexico.

CHAPTER III: Cuauhtémoc's Early Years

Cuauhtémoc (Kwow-TAY-mok) Cárdenas was born on May 1, 1934, and both the first name and his date of birth have symbolic importance to all Mexicans. Cuauhtémoc was the last Aztec emperor to resist Cortés and the invading Spaniards in 1521. A statue of this Indian hero stands at one of Mexico City's busiest intersections. (There is no monument to the conquistador, Cortés, anywhere in the city.) And May First is Labor Day, the workers' holiday, in countries with socialist orientations.

In fact, the 1934 president-to-be was presiding over an official May Day celebration the morning his son was born. Lázaro's friend, Francisco Múgica, was the first to know and tell the new father. Múgica became Cuauhtémoc's godfather, and he witnessed the official registration of the boy's birth. The boy's father had intended to name his son Álvaro, after ex-president Obregón, because of the fond memories Lázaro had of serving under Obregón during the revolution. But suddenly, he decided on Cuauhtémoc, the Aztec hero, and Cuauhtémoc it was.

Cuauhtémoc came into his parents' lives at a chaotic time. For centuries the leader of Mexico had resided in the lavish palace in Chapultepec Park in Mexico City. But Lázaro Cárdenas had decided to refurbish a modest compound on the edge of the park. He christened the house "Los Pinos," after the garden where he had met his future wife, Amalia Solórzano, and Los Pinos has been Mexico's presidential home ever since. In the upheaval of the first months of the presidency and moving into a new home, the new baby, Cuauhtémoc, had no crib. His mother fashioned a bed in a large coat box so the baby could be easily moved. So from the beginning, this was to be no ordinary life—from an outsider's perspective.

Recently asked what if felt like then to be the child of Mexico's most honored politician, Cuauhtémoc replied that he didn't really know. This man was simply his father. By age three or four, he would sometimes ride with his father to Chapultepec Castle, often with other government dignitaries along, to the offices where the business of government was conducted. Cuauhtémoc would play a while in the palace and then be taken home. And it was not a pampered and lonely life at home because at Los Pinos, Lázaro boarded several children of men working in his administration. Cuauhtémoc began attending school with them as just another of the boys.

Los Pinos, a modern mansion now, was almost a small, rustic ranch in the heart of the Mexican capital in the late 1930s. There were riding paths and a small stable where Cuauhtémoc's father taught him to ride, and in a small, unheated pool, his father took him swimming each morning. He remembers Lázaro Cárdenas then, not as a nation's president, but as an affectionate father who always shared his son's daily life. When as a young boy, Cuauhtémoc wanted to be a bullfighter, like small boys want to grow up to be cowboys or Superman, his father began taking him to the bull fights until the boy outgrew the youthful notion.

Cuauhtémoc's earliest memories are of Los Pinos as a playground, but the family also owned a ranch near Cuernavaca where aunts and uncles, cousins and grandparents often gathered. It was here where he began to pick up on his father's genuine love for agriculture, ranching, and country life. He remembers going with his father to check gardens and to prune orchard trees around the ranch. Lázaro also had a cattle breeding project there, crossing Swiss and native Cebú breeds, trying to improve his herds. He was personally involved with those who lived and worked on his ranch and in the region. Outdoor experience became a natural part of the life Cuauhtémoc shared with his father.

The close-knit family has always been Mexico's most important cultural unit. But while young Cuauhtémoc was getting to know this man as father, this president, as father of his country, was about to make one of the most significant decisions in Mexico's history. On March 18, 1938, Lázaro Cárdenas expropriated all Mexico's oil producing properties from foreign, private owners—all British and American companies—and reasserted Mexico's sovereign right of ownership of all her natural resources.

For years these foreign companies had exploited the oil reserves and the native workers. Foreign owners were rich, and Mexican laboring families lived in poverty conditions. Mexican oil was even sold to Mexicans at a higher price than was charged for it in the United States. When the oil workers' union went on strike for better working conditions and better wages, Cárdenas supported them. Arrogant owners refused to bargain, and President Cárdenas seized their property in the name of state, fulfilling to the letter of the law Article 123 of the Constitution of 1917.

A wave of national pride and celebration swept over all of Mexico. The nation had asserted its sovereign rights to self-determination. For over 400 years, Mexico had been treated as someone else's property, even after independence in 1810. In reclaiming control of oil resources, the Mexican people came together as a free and independent nation. With this decree, Lázaro Cárdenas became a national hero, and the date, March 18, is now a traditional holiday in many parts of Mexico.

Oil companies demanded U.S. military intervention, but President Franklin Roosevelt honored Mexico's national right and asked only that the expelled owners be given financial compensation. Mexicans in every part of the country lined up to donate all personal wealth, from jewelry and savings to farm animals and agricultural crops, in order to help pay this national debt of honor. A well-known photo shows Cuauhtémoc, not quite four years old, at the Palace of Fine Arts in Mexico City. He is with his father and many other school children, donating his piggy bank to the cause. Of course, most of this action was a symbolic display of national unity, but it was also the first time Cuauhtémoc was at the focus of national politics and history.

At age five, Cuauhtémoc accompanied his father on the first of a lifetime of trips into the Mexican countryside to meet face to face with the rural people about their problems. He saw the back country and the ruins of his country's Mayan past, and he began to be aware of Mexico's rich history and culture. He was unaware that his father had recently taken thousands of acres of sisal plantation land in Yucatan from rich hacienda families and put them under the control of the Mayan population that had slaved on the land for generations. During his administration as president, Lázaro Cárdenas changed the hacendado system of land ownership and worker exploitation into the village *ejido* system of agricultural management. Not always a success in bettering economic life for country people, by 1940, Cárdenas had overseen the distribution of 45 million acres of agricultural land from private ownership by a few rich individual families to *ejidos* of village people who actually lived on and worked the land. He distributed more than twice the amount of land than all previous administrations combined. This action created a big change in the way of life for many of Mexico's country peasants.

It wasn't until age six, at the end of his father's presidency, that Cuauhtémoc began to understand on a personal level that his father was an extraordinary individual, that he affected many people's lives in profound ways, and not just his young son's. Although he would pass the presidency to Ávila Camacho (1940-1946), Lázaro Cárdenas would serve, and be venerated by, the Mexican people for decades to come. For Cuauhtémoc, he would not only be a full-time father, but also best friend, wisest mentor, and the most shining example of the values to live by: tolerance and kindness toward others, personal honesty and honor, and selfless service to fellow countrymen.

Coinciding with World War II (1939-45), Cuauhtémoc's early grade school years were a time of upheaval and change. There was real concern that Japan would try to invade the United States by way of Mexico, and his father was appointed military commander of the Pacific region to oversee the coastal defense. Lázaro had to move around the country frequently, and during three years Cuauhtémoc was enrolled in at least six different schools in three different states and the federal district. Fortunately, a good memory and a gift for scientific reasoning helped him retain lessons well, and he kept pace with changing classmates. Perhaps the constant situation of being "the new

kid in school" contributed to his quiet, almost timid personality that is still part of his character today. Yet he made
friends easily, once classmates got over the novelty that
Cuauhtémoc was the son of an ex-president.

Some early classmates became life-long friends, but
as Cuauhtémoc grew older, his truest friend would be his
father. While Lázaro served the administrations of subse-
quent presidents, he still had time for his son, often taking
Cuauhtémoc with him into whatever part of Mexico his
work called him. They liked to ride horseback and swim,
and Cuauhtémoc's interest in natural resources and ecology, in agriculture and country life, grew stronger through
the experiences he shared with his father. Lázaro was
also an avid reader and loved to talk about Mexico's history and his own experiences during the revolution. Discussion over the dinner table in the evening was a large
part of family life during Cuauhtémoc's childhood.

As Lázaro continued to work for the government, the
family settled in Mexico City, and Cuauhtémoc attended
Williams School in the colonia (suburb) of Mexcoac until age fourteen. His natural inclination toward practical
reasoning and logic influenced his interest in science, and
especially in chemistry. Family vacations were spent in the
countryside of Michoacán with grandparents and other relatives, rekindling his interest in the outdoors, agriculture
and ranching, and in camping and wildlife.

It was a time of family life and growth for Cuauhtémoc,
but a time of economic boom in Mexico. Official government policy into the late 1950s was focused on rapid in-
dustrialization of the nation through private ownership of
business and manufacturing. A growing class of *nouveau
riche* (new rich) businessmen began to emerge in Mexico's culture, and the ties between the single ruling party,
PRI, and the special economic interests of these entrepre-
neurs became a way of life. The government, as a major
business interest itself, built roads, oil refineries, railroads,
and industrial sites. Work and materials were never put
up to competitive bidding, but were funneled through PRI
to party friends and family as over-priced contracts that al-

lowed certain individuals involved to make huge personal profits and to pay back those in government who helped the process along. By the end of the Alemán administration (1946-1952), the process of the rich getting richer and the living standards of the poor rarely improving, was solidly entrenched in Mexico. The common citizen could not make a decent living on an honest salary, so the taking of bribes (*mordidas*) to expedite any kind of business, from getting a building permit to getting a union plumber to show up promptly, became common cultural practice. The next president's administration was more honest (Ruiz Cortines, 1952-1958), but many of Mexico's political and economic problems were already too big to change.

In 1949 Lázaro Cárdenas had retired into private life, and the family moved back to their home state of Michoacán. Cuauhtémoc was enrolled in the college preparatory school, San Nicolás, in the small city of Morelia. Moving from the urban bustle of Mexico City to the small town life of Morelia was a big cultural change as well, but it only served to reinforce Cuauhtémoc's interest in nature and the physical elements and in Mexico's varied ways of life.

His school interests had moved naturally from chemistry to math and physical science. He found a satisfaction working with concrete laws of physics, and coupled with his interest in nature, he began to consider civil engineering as a profession. His father encouraged him in these interests. Lázaro had never tried to steer his son toward a particular career. But he had been very clear in his desire that Cuauhtémoc stay out of Mexican party politics and the military. While Lázaro's skills in these fields had made him Mexico's most respected leader, he wasn't exempt from the personal costs of civil service. There was constant self-sacrifice, and pressure and worry brought on by national responsibility and political conflict.

Taking his father's advice, Cuauhtémoc moved back to Mexico City in 1951 to study civil engineering as a life career. And except in support of his father, he would stay out of national party politics until well after Lázaro Cárdenas' death in 1970.

CHAPTER IV: Into Turbulent Years

In 1951 Cuauhtémoc returned to Mexico City to begin his formal studies in civil engineering. The nature of water had always held a personal attraction for him, and the study of dam construction and river ecology became his professional focus. Cuauhtémoc was a member of the last class to begin and finish studies together at the Palacio de Minería, the College of Mines, that was part of the National Autonomous University of Mexico (UNAM), located in Tacuba, a colonia of the growing Mexican capital. Here he revived friendships from secondary school and began new friendships that would evolve into close professional and political alliances over the years. Cuauhtémoc was an excellent student, and a concentration on the finite laws of science and math helped make this time of his life a comfortable and easy part of growing up. Sharing daily life with his parents at the family home in Colonia Guadalupe Inn, another part of Mexico City, was a stable and quiet part of college life as well.

In contrast to Cuauhtémoc's student life, global politics and international relations were heating up. The 1950s saw the Cold War intensify as the capitalist western world began an idealistic showdown with the Soviet communist eastern world. The Korean War (1950-1953) was on, the atomic arms race had begun, and McCarthyism, an authoritarian political repression in the name of fighting communist conspiracy, was on the rise in the United States. In the geopolitical struggle between East and West for world domination, smaller countries were often treated like squares on the world chess board. Mexico, with its conflicting constitutional mix of capitalism and socialism, walked a political tightrope, trying to maintain its global independence. But with the rest of Latin America, Mexico shared a trend toward leftist socialist policies and had a justifiable fear and resentment for "Yankee Imperialism."

In 1954 the American Central Intelligence Agency instigated a "coup d'etat"—an overthrow of President Jacobo Arbenz of Guatemala, Mexico's closest southern neighbor, fearing that government's communist ties. Arbenz had been democratically elected, and he advocated agrarian reform programs inspired by Lázaro Cárdenas' administration in Mexico years before. The installation of a U.S.–backed dictator to replace Arbenz in Guatemala inspired political protest throughout Latin America. The protest in Mexico would be Cuauhtémoc Cárdenas' first personal experience with political action.

Along with other students from UNAM, Cárdenas helped organize, and then he headed, the National Protest of Mexican Students Against the Invasion of Guatemala. One of only two students from the college of engineering to actively participate in this national movement, he began to forge contacts with other students and leaders in different professional studies who shared some of his own political views and interests.

The East-West conflict inspired many international conferences, particularly of Third World nations trying to strike a balance between Soviet influence and American imperialism. One such conference was named the World Peace Movement, co-founded by Lázaro Cárdenas. He received the Stalin Peace Prize in 1955 for his political stands and influence. He also helped to instigate the Latin American Conference on Peace, Free Trade, and National Sovereignty, and his own son, Cuauhtémoc, would eventually be a participant at that conference's 1961 convention.

In Mexico itself these same political factions, capitalism and socialism, struggled in the form of business and land owners versus labor union activists. There was also a rapid growth of rural populations that wanted a revival of socialist agrarian land reform again. Inflation made ordinary workers' pay worth less and less, and in 1957 and 1958, this led to railroad, oil worker, electrician, and telegraphers union strikes all across the nation as unionists demanded better wages. The Mexican government, fearing that too much communist influence in the unions could provoke U.S. interference, sent the army in to break the strikes. The government arrested union leaders and over 10,000 workers. Meanwhile, only the personal influence of Lázaro Cárdenas and President Ruiz Cortines stopped the expulsion of a small group of Cuban dissidents hiding in Mexico. They were under the leadership of a young revolutionary named Fidel Castro.

The Cuban Revolution in 1959 drew western hemisphere politics into even deeper turmoil. In its first year of existence, the new revolutionary Cuban government was not formally communistic. It was considered throughout Latin America a great example of the struggle for global independence. As 1960 approached, young Mexican intellectuals, Cuauhtémoc Cárdenas among them, were looking for a "third way" between U.S. and U.S.S.R. pressure politics. They felt that the best way to promote Mexico's independent and socialist policies was to support and defend the Cuban Revolution. Six months after the revolt, former Mexican President Lázaro Cárdenas stood beside Fidel Castro on a balcony overlooking old Havana's main plaza where they watched the people's parade celebrating new land reform in Cuba. Beside them both was the young Cuauhtémoc Cárdenas.

But just as his appearance at the Palace of Fine Arts at age four, supporting his father's expropriation of Mexico's oil fields in 1938, had been largely symbolic, so was this display. While Mexican and Caribbean politics had been heating up in the late 1950s, Cuauhtémoc had kept a cool arm's distance from the international furor, quietly advancing in his professional studies in civil engineering. Although he would attend the World Peace Movement conferences in France and India as his father's personal representative, he was primarily in Europe on a grant from Mexico's Ministry of the Exterior, arranged for him by President Ruiz Cortines.

After graduating from UNAM, Cuauhtémoc spent most of 1957 and 1958 visiting and studying industrial and hydroelectric projects in France, Germany, and Italy. Ultimately, his life goals were still personal, professional, and focused on his home state of Michoacán. His father had long pursued an old dream of establishing a vast industrial and hydroelectric project in the Las Balsas region of Michoacán. The grant from the Ministry of the Interior es-

tablished Cuauhtémoc as a member of the new Tepalcate-
pec Commission, and the sites he visited in Europe were
examples of what both Cárdenas men hoped to create at
home.

When Cuauhtémoc returned to Mexico in February of
1959, he headed a small construction company that he
and school friends had established during their last year
in college. But his interests were now focused on large-
scale engineering projects like those he had seen recently
in Europe, and their business company was dissolved.
Then in the spring of 1959, at the age of 25, personal
dreams were realized when the new president, Adolfo
López Mateos (1958-1964) commissioned the Río Balsas
Study. Cuauhtémoc Cárdenas was appointed a Subsecretary of Water Resources and put in charge of studying
the Balsa River gorge and the regional watershed that
crossed seven states. His job was to assess possible hydroelectric improvements, the need for schools, sanitation
facilities, and urban development projects in this area of
Mexico.

In traditional Mexican fashion, Cuauhtémoc called on
the services of former classmates and friends he had
made during political activities supporting Guatemalan independence and the new World Peace Movement. These
friends helped create a two-year study of the region. Men
such as César Buenrostro, Leonel Durán, and Alfonso
Vaca joined Cárdenas' executive committee. They were
young professionals in other social, industrial, and bureaucratic careers eager to help make this project a success.
They would also become Cárdenas' life-long friends and
his most important political supporters later in life.

This work took Cuauhtémoc all over Michoacán, Jalisco,
Guerrero, and other states, inspecting infrastructures such
as roads and bridges and railroads, and measuring natural resources such as river flows, mining possibilities, and
timber stands. By jeep, Cárdenas visited towns, villages,
and backwater pueblos, getting to know local representatives, who in turn knew their personal parts of the Río
Balsas region and could help assess the area's needs.

In a natural style inherited from his father, Cuauhtémoc was getting to know personally the heart of a "real" Mexico and the everyday peasant life in the region. Common people of the country were not abstract ideas discussed by political VIPs in Mexico City offices, but flesh and blood fellow Mexicans that Cuauhtémoc Cárdenas worked with hand-in-hand every day.

Despite his professional responsibilities, Cuauhtémoc still found time to participate in his father's political activities. He attended the Latin American Conference on Peace, and he had accompanied Lázaro to Cuba in July 1959 and again in 1960 before the Bay of Pigs debacle that once again heightened tensions in the Caribbean, driving Castro into political conspiracy with Russia. Within Mexico itself, Lázaro Cárdenas was still totally committed to the socialist ideals of the Mexican Revolution. Rural people still needed land to live on, and labor unions were not anti-government enemies as so many in the PRI bureaucracy claimed. He believed that they addressed the real problems of the urban workers. Regarding Cuba, his own Mexico, and all of Latin America, Lázaro Cárdenas proclaimed that the problem was not communism. It was poverty.

The Latin American Conference on Peace, Free Trade, and National Sovereignty in 1961 justifiably encouraged each county to unite its leftist political factions to defend the Cuban Revolution and to protect themselves against U.S. yankee imperialism. The Bay of Pigs Invasion, sponsored by the CIA in 1961, was violently protested throughout Latin America, particularly by Lázaro Cárdenas, who was not allowed by his own government to visit Cuba again that year for fear of the political upheaval it might cause, along with unpredictable U.S. retaliation. Again, a fever of *Cardenísmo* stirred the people's passions. *Cardenísmo* advocated complete agrarian reform and a government defense of national resources. It proposed strong government control over bourgeois capitalism, a firm support of Cuban independence, and loud anti-Americanism.

In August 1961, young Mexican intellectuals formally

created the Mexican chapter of the National Liberation Movement (MLN–Movimiento Liberacion Nacíonal) under this banner of *Cardenísmo*. It was strictly a pacifist movement and intended to stay independent of any specific political party. It wasn't concerned with the internal politics of PRI and the federal government or in the international struggle between East-West ideologies. The new movement's supporters, including Cuauhtémoc and many of his friends and fellow professionals working on the Río Balsas Project, went into other parts of Mexico, attempting to unite labor unionists, disenchanted PRI members, socialists, communists, and independents under the *Cardenísmo* ideals. Cuauhtémoc dedicated all of 1962 to MLN organizing.

Lázaro Cárdenas and the MLN also worked for the release of political prisoners, particularly the leaders of the railroad strike who had been jailed after the 1959 strikes. Visiting these prisoners in Lecumberri Prison with his father, Cuauhtémoc was educated in other aspects of Mexican politics and its repercussions on vocal minority dissidents. PRI and the federal government actually seemed afraid of free speech and real political opposition, and its advocates were jailed as threats to national stability. Demanding more land distribution to the poor, as well as criticizing the government for favoring pro-American capitalism over the rights and wages of the poor, the National Liberation Movement was a thorn in the side of PRI and President López Mateos. The MLN influenced the Mexican government into maintaining an independent stance of support for Cuba's struggle and compelled new education initiatives in Mexico's rural areas. López Mateos also distributed more new land to peasants than had any president except Cárdenas himself.

The mid-1960s continued to be a time of rising political tension around the world, and not just in Mexico. Student and workers' movements, especially in France, Czechoslovakia, the United States, and China agitated for more freedom and rights. Regional armed conflicts evolved into wars like in Vietnam. Idealists raged against perceived corruption and deception in many national governments, which in turn, became increasingly restrictive and violent in response. Mexico was not exempt from political problems. In 1963, PRI politician, Carlos Medrazo, suggested democratic reform within the PRI party, and he was removed from leadership. In the state of San Luis Potosí, maverick PRI politician, Dr. Salvador Nava was the first to win a municipal office unsupported by party leadership, but he was denied the governorship a year later, beaten, and imprisoned. Political progress toward democracy was slow and personally costly to the brave voices speaking out in its support.

By the end of the López Mateos presidency, both Lázaro and Cuauhtémoc Cárdenas needed change and relief in their intense lives. Personal, as well as national, situations were changing. Despite criticism from followers, Lázaro Cárdenas accepted the Chief Executive Directorship of the new Balsas River Commission. This was the huge hydroelectric project in the Las Balsas region he had envisioned long ago and which was developed in the study done by his son. It seemed to some that he was being bought off by the PRI and the federal government to silence troublesome leftist criticism. But Lázaro was already nearly 70 years old and in failing health. This offer was a chance to realize an old dream. And besides, he argued, the position would allow him to defend Michoacán's natural resources and its people against exploitation by foreign interests.

He asked his son, Cuauhtémoc, to join him as one of the principal engineers on the project. It was a way to get away from ever-growing political tensions in Mexico before becoming another of its victims. For Cuauhtémoc, this was the opportunity to return to professional practice, and he eventually became the resident engineer and Director of Studies of the Río Balsas Commission. And finally, it was a chance to focus more on his personal life, too. Family and professional life were calling.

CHAPTER V: The Professional Years

Although Cárdenas dedicated 1962 to organizing for the MLN, he also refocused on his personal and professional life. That same year he helped to found, and then presided over, the Mexican Society of Planning (Soceidad Mexicana de Planificacíon). This was a non-government association of professionals who were engineers, architects, lawyers, and businessmen with a general interest in the technical and ordered development of natural resources and urban planning. They planned and promoted projects to build infrastructures like roads and bridges and dams that would improve the standards of living throughout the country. During his presidency of the society, Cárdenas developed professional and personal relationships with many men rising in the worlds of Mexican business and government bureaucracy, like Jóse López Portillo, who would later influence Cárdenas' unforeseen political future.

As Cárdenas took up his engineering career, he also experienced profound personal changes. In 1963 he married Celeste Batal, a young women of Portuguese and Spanish descent who had moved to Mexico with her parents shortly after World War II. They met at a party at the home of Cuauhtémoc's cousin, who was Celeste's friend and classmate. After a friendship through the school years, they married in Mexico City, and life changes came quickly.

While expecting their first child, Cuauhtémoc became the Resident Engineer for the construction of La Villita Dam near the mouth of the Las Balsas River. He was also Director of Studies of the Las Balsas Commission, designing the giant construction project. He began his work under the Chief Executive leadership of his father, Lázaro. Cuauhtémoc moved to the small village of Melchor Ocampo in the spring of 1964 to oversee the massive Las Balsas project. Shortly after the birth of their first son, christened Lázaro in honor of his grandfather, Celeste joined her husband in the tiny town of about 2,500 fishermen and farmers. The town was without electricity, and its only access was a landing strip for small planes and undeveloped roads which were nearly impassable in the rainy season.

In Melchor Ocampo, new natural resource development began, and career and family flourished. Cárdenas would be Resident Engineer from 1964 to 1967, fully engaged in the straight-forward, tangible tasks of civil engineering, overseeing the construction of the dam, tunnels, bridges, and roads. He also worked on the port facilities and a new workers' urban site around Melchor Ocampo that would quickly grow into the city of over 50,000 inhabitants. La Villita Dam was part of a huge project intended for multiple uses: for agricultural irrigation, hydroelectric generation, and as a transportation link between Michoacán and the bordering state of Guerrero where another dam, part of the same project, was being built in the "tierra caliente," the hot country of the tropical mountains. This giant project was an example of the Mexican government trying to fulfill the socialist ideals of *Cardenísmo* in its most honorable sense, using its authority and responsible bureaucratic control to develop national resources to better the regional standard of living for thousands of rural Mexicans.

While fully involved in his professional career in 1966, Cárdenas also became president of the Technical Advisory Council for the National Confederation of Peasants (CNC–Confederacíon Nacional de Campesinos). It is a political union of small farmers and *ejido* members, much like a labor union, founded by Lázaro Cárdenas in 1958 to represent the interests of agrarian policy within the PRI government bureaucracy. By filling this official position from 1966 to 1968, Cuauhtémoc was automatically considered to be a member of PRI, although there had never been a formal application or an acceptance of these credentials. In 1968 he also became a member of the steering committee of the Inter-American Society of Planning (SIAP–Sociedad InterAmericana de Planificacíon). By now a highly respected engineer and government functionary, Cuauhtémoc Cárdenas could have been considered a member of the ruling class in Mexico, serving in several official positions and overseeing a part of the nation's development.

With many official interests, Cárdenas' focus on life and career remained at the town of Melchor Oampo, directing the Las Balsas project. In 1967 a second son was born and named Cuauhtémoc, after his father. Family life, so important in all of Mexican society and especially in the Cárdenas family, continued to grow strong roots and to flourish. Much as his own father had, Cuauhtémoc involved his children with the travels and day-to-day activities of his work as they began to grow up. Family life became rich and rewarding, in part, because of the common interests and involvement his wife, Celeste, has sustained and shared over the years. Cárdenas' warm and secure family life enhanced and enlivened his professional life through the 1960s.

While the decade was busy, yet calm and simple for Cárdenas, it was a turbulent era throughout the world. The East-West Cold War was at its height, intensified by the Vietnam War, the Arab-Israeli conflict, and the space race. Rapid change was taking place in culture, technology, and political perspective worldwide. Differences in cultural perspectives and values widened between generations and became issues of more conflict. In 1968 there were massive student riots at universities in the United States, France, England, and other countries. Internal politics and cultural tensions were high in Mexico as well.

Students at the National University (UNAM) mobilized to protest army occupation of several campuses where organizers were calling for a repeal of part of the Penal Code called the "crime of opinion," which made it a crime to criticize the government. They also called for release of political prisoners and the dismissal of the Mexico City chief of police. The activists asked for "public dialogue" with a government which now generally worked in private sessions and secrecy. The president and friends were far removed from the voices of regular people in the street. In a loud, almost unconscious way, these students and other activists first vocalized the growing problem in Mexico—

the need for democratization and power sharing.

By October 1968, President Gustavo Díaz Ordaz (1964-1970) was convinced of a communist conspiracy to destabilize Mexico. Mexico was scheduled to host the summer Olympics at the end of the month, a chance to showcase the country as a rising, prosperous, modern nation. He would not see Mexico shamed or blackmailed by a vocal opposition of brainwashed youth and citizen outlaws. On October 2, a massive demonstration march began at the university and headed for the Plaza of Three Cultures in the heart of Mexico City. There, the Díaz Ordaz administration responded to the Student Movement with violent force. The army opened fire in the full plaza, massacring between 300 and 400 people. Then responsibility was quickly covered up and propagandized. The Olympics went on during the following weeks, and the new democratic movement in Mexico had been crushed into silence.

At this time, both the ex-president Cárdenas and his son Cuauhtémoc were still deeply involved in the real and practical tasks of hydroelectric and urban development on Las Balsas River in Michoacán. Perhaps Lázaro Cárdenas, Mexico's consummate politician of the left, simply understood when to distance himself (and his destabilizing influence) from situations too volatile to control. Cuauhtémoc, earlier in 1968, had also resigned his position with the CNC advisory council when attacks in the press challenged his ideas on managing the nation's natural resources. He quickly distanced himself from what elements of turbulent national policies that he could. Had either man been an active player in the troubled political chaos of those years in Mexico City, the violence may have focused on and consumed them. As it was, business and family life kept them busy in Michoacán.

In retrospect, Cuauhtémoc Cárdenas sees October 2, 1968, as the first major division between the PRI-controlled government of Mexico and the common people that it supposedly represented and protected. It had attacked when confronted with the people's political opposition. In the Plaza of Three Cultures, the seeds of today's democratic movement were planted, even though it had been temporarily stunned into silence by political violence.

As 1970 approached, Cuauhtémoc Cárdenas officially left the Las Balsas Commission to become Subdirector of Las Truchas Iron and Steel Works Project. This was just another part of the Balsas development and part of his father's old dream for the region. It was to be a steel works that utilized the electrical energy produced at La Villita Dam and the mineral ores mined in that part of Mexico. It took until 1971 to get this part of the project up and running. There was opposition to the project from private enterprise concerns already manufacturing steel. They were against government competition. Along with Director Adolfo Videalba, Cárdenas often presented project plans to the Interior Secretary, the National Finance Minister, and even to the President, seeking support and funds for their project's advance. Through his professional capacity as engineer and project bureaucrat, Cárdenas came to know President Díaz Ordaz and his hand-picked successor, Luis Echeverría. Cárdenas necessarily accompanied these men when they toured parts of the Las Balsas project, but the relationship was always strictly on a professional and business basis, never about government or party politics or personal lives.

Abruptly, on October 19, 1970, former President Lázaro Cárdenas died. There was a time of national mourning, and since his death, Lázaro Cárdenas has become Mexico's most revered past president. He is remembered as a true leader of the common people, distributor of land to the poor and savior of the nation's natural resources. His life and influence on the nation of Mexico are seen in heroic proportions by many. His death was a tremendous national loss, but it was even more devastating to his son.

Theirs had been a deep and constant relationship since Cuauhtémoc's birth. They played together, experienced Mexico and its people together. They lived, worked, and campaigned for people's causes together. They were business partners and best friends, as well as father and son. At age 36, in the middle of his busy professional career and an active and growing family life, this loss was the hardest Cuauhtémoc Cárdenas has ever had to experience. Yet life must go on, and it did, but the father's legacies of family values and political principles live on yet today in the political philosophies and lifestyle of his son.

CHAPTER VI: Early Political Lessons

After the death of Cárdenas' father, outgoing President Díaz Ordaz and President-elect Luis Echeverría travelled to Michoacán to pay last respects to this nationally respected family. Echeverría renamed the once-small village of Melchor Ocampo at the mouth of Las Balsas River Ciudad Lázaro Cárdenas in honor of the past president. The new president-to-be also asked Cuauhtémoc and his widowed mother to make a promotional tour with him along the Jalisco and Michoacán coastline. Traditionally, between election in July and taking office in December, the new Mexican president makes a victory campaign through parts of the country, telling people how his *sexenio*, his six-year term in office, will be different than his predecessor's. Making public appearances with regionally well-known and popular business and civic leaders helps create an aura of support and trust for the next administration.

The presence of Cárdenas family members at this emotional time in the political history of the nation no doubt enhanced Echeverría's regional popularity. Later, he asked Cárdenas to accompany him on swings through the Yucatan peninsula as well. Cárdenas was the current director of a new commission of studies, similar to that of Las Balsas, for rivers in the states of Campeche, Tabasco, and Chiapas. He accompanied Echeverría to this region as a technical advisor. While this was a respectable and primarily a business relationship, it was also a chance for Echeverría to size up Cuauhtémoc Cárdenas as a business leader, as a PRI bureaucracy member, and as a political ally.

While Cárdenas seemed to have easy access to the president's office in the early 1970s, he was still primarily involved in the Las Truchas Steel Works Project. He enjoyed the work, but difficulties and differences with Director Videalba over management arose. Las Truchas was costing more in government spending than it was producing, using coal imported from Columbia to generate needed power and contributing to Mexico's growing foreign debt. Cárdenas asked President Echeverría to be relieved of his duties as subdirector, but his resignation was rejected. Cárdenas continued as subdirector until 1974, but he focused on the urban development problems of the fast-growing city of Lázaro Cárdenas.

Except in representing his father at the Latin American Conference on Peace and Free Trade, and as a member of the National Liberation Movement in the early 1960s, Cárdenas had kept out of Mexican political life for almost twenty years, respecting the wishes and warnings of his father. But in Cuauhtémoc's acquaintance with Echeverría, he had heard this new president speak about more freedom within the PRI, saying that candidates chosen for office by popular consent would be respected and accepted. At this time, in part, because of dissatisfaction with his professional situation, Cárdenas began to consider seeking the governorship of his home state of Michoacán. He explored the possibility by seeking and finding much local support within the state. Considering his family background and his obvious personal involvement in the state's development of infrastructure and jobs, this was no surprise. However, access to the president's audience suddenly became impossible. Echeverría seemed too busy to discuss these things, and essentially, the silent message being sent was that the political doors were not open to Cárdenas.

Reaching public office still seemed like a true possibility, and Cárdenas took the president at his word that all candidates would get equal opportunity. He proceeded with his political plans. He once again tendered his resignation as Subdirector of the Las Truchas project, but this time he took it to long-time associate, José López Portillo who was now Minister of Finance. Cárdenas had worked with López Portillo ten years before on the Mexican Society of Planning and as Secretary of Housing when Cárdenas was promoting the Las Truchas project. His resignation was accepted this time by a friend who would later figure prominently in Cárdenas's political career by unexpectedly becoming the next designated president.

In 1974, however, López Portillo was just a figurehead

cabinet member who gave Cárdenas a small chance to pursue political office. Later that same year, in a closed party meeting, President Echeverría gave his *dedazo* to Carlos Torres Manza, then Secretary of Industry and Commerce, to be the next official PRI candidate (and therefore, presumed elected) as governor of Michoacán. Cárdenas had not even been invited to the meeting. He was not yet an accepted member of the PRI inner circle. In angry response, Cárdenas wrote and had published in state newspapers a public protest against a party and its leader who goes back on his promises.

The governorship denied, Cárdenas accepted the directorship of the Federal Commission of Ciudad Lázaro Cárdenas, a position like regional manager of this industrial development site. Cárdenas resumed his professional life and made no waves in the political swamp of Mexico's national politics, keeping the Las Truchas directorship until 1976. Privately, his assessment of President Echeverría was that the man could have done more for the people. Inflation and debt increased during his administration, and government continued to manage its business concerns with careless and extravagant waste. Echeverría had no will to implement policies that he said he supported.

It was a lesson Cárdenas took to heart. For him, this was a prime example of Mexican politicians' actions not being consistent with their promises. It was a primary reason why average Mexicans were becoming more cynical and losing faith in government. Historically and instinctively, Cárdenas also understood that he could effect no changes in Mexico's political process by being a loud dissident outside the system. Events in 1968 had proven that, and in 1974 the political doors were indeed closed to him. That is, until the unexpected *destape* of the next president.

In January of 1976, the anointed successor to the presidency, José López Portillo (1976-1982), made a traditional campaign appearance in Michoacán. Having known Cárdenas in various official capacities over the previous fifteen years, he proposed that Cárdenas become a PRI candidate for the senate. Mexico's government has a Chamber of Deputies and a Senate as law-making bodies, but like all other offices, the PRI candidate/office-holder is hand-picked by the president as elections roll around. The ruling houses merely rubber stamp approval of the president's agenda.

Cárdenas' first reply was that he would rather serve Mexico in administrative positions as he had at Las Truchas and on other commissions studying Mexico's natural resource development. But the president-elect suggested that running for the senate was a good way for Cárdenas to gain valuable electoral experience. This was a kind of *dedazo* for Cárdenas to a rather minor position in the mechanisms of Mexico's government.

While he could see this candidacy as a way inside the political bureaucracy of PRI, he also saw this opportunity as a chance to link himself completely with the people and the state of Michoacán. As a reward or step up the bureaucratic ladder, senate seats are often given to presidential friends who may or may not have a real relationship with the regional voters they are to represent. But Cárdenas had a family tradition and a day-to-day working relationship with the people of Michoacán. With the senate seat assured and his ability to represent the state of no doubt, he simply could have gone to office in Mexico City. But he made a campaign unusual for senate candidates, a "real" campaign. He didn't use the PRI political machine in the bigger cities of the state, making quick junkets for public appearances and closed-door party sessions, granting other insiders government jobs.

Following his father's campaign tradition, Cuauhtémoc went out to meet the people of the state—so many of whom he already knew while a laboring engineer working daily with the citizens who build roads and manage city facilities and run businesses. With the help and transportation means of local friends, Cárdenas visited all 113 municipalities (counties) of the state. He would know his constituency, and they would know their representative. While the senate seat was a place inside the entrenched workings of the PRI political network, it would have personal advantages, too. Doing PRI work in the senate, Cárdenas would come to know Porfirio Muñoz Ledo, then president of the PRI party, and many other high position holders who would become friends, colleagues, and eventual political allies.

This was also Cárdenas' first opportunity to take the fight for democratic ideals inside the party. He believed in face-to-face knowledge of, and experience with, the fellow countrymen he represented. He believed in selfless and honest representation and in socialist policies that truly improve the national standard of living. And he would begin to build his political future on this foundation.

Following elections in July, Cárdenas would hold the senate seat until 1982, but he was also given more far-reaching responsibilities when López Portillo named him Subsecretary of Forestry and Wildlife in the Department of Agriculture and Water Resources, a cabinet member position in the government. For the next four years, he directed policy concerning Mexico's natural resource development, a field of knowledge in which he had twenty years of experience.

Having worked within the party system, fulfilling his role as a capable functionary, Cárdenas was given the official sanction, the *dedazo*, in 1980 to return to Michoacán to run as the PRI candidate for governor. Cuauhtémoc Cárdenas was on his way to becoming a key figure in PRI party bureaucracy and the inner workings of Mexican government.

CHAPTER VII: During the Cárdenas Governorship

Announced as the PRI candidate for governor of Michoacán in 1980, Cárdenas was now seen by party leaders as one of the cogs in the standard bureaucratic mechanisms of Mexican politics. But once again, his campaign would be anything but ordinary party networking. With the help of Javier Ovando, friend and long-time colleague who had managed his senate campaign, Cárdenas once again took his father's style of electioneering directly to the people of the state. He was in every municipality, reestablishing personal contact and political ties with villagers and farmers, as well as with business professionals and workers in Morelia, Uruapan, and the other cities of the state. As high office-holder in Mexico's national government, few could claim such direct and personal involvement and such deep roots in the history and culture, the business and government of a region and its people as Cuauhtémoc Cárdenas in Michoacán.

Cárdenas served as governor from 1980 to the end of 1986. He began his term while Mexico's national economy was extravagantly financed by López Portillo's policy of borrowing from other countries, using as collateral the estimated worth of newly discovered oil reserves in the Bay of Campeche. With funds distributed to Michoacán, Cárdenas created the Institute of Culture and the Institute of Sports, promoting healthy lifestyle and cultural activity throughout the state. Other public works were also begun, providing jobs and improvements in living conditions. Later, as Mexico's economic situation deteriorated, all these programs would be cut as an austerity measure.

During his governorship, Cárdenas also enforced the federal laws against liquor sales from Saturday evening till Monday morning, and he prohibited cockfights, a popular spectator sport, at county fairs. Much in the way his father tried to "de-alcoholize and defanaticize" the state's population in the 1930s, Cuauhtémoc sought to tone down violence and crime that tend to be fueled by alcoholic celebration and sports gambling. In some circles, this earned Cárdenas the image of a conservative prude and teetotaler, but crime and accident statistics showed clear improvement once these laws were enforced.

Cárdenas himself has never smoked and rarely drinks alcoholic beverages, and his busy life had never allowed time for entertainment like cockfights. But enforcement of laws already enacted was not an attempt by Cárdenas to change others' values and habits. This was a first step toward upholding already established standards with honest enforcement and clean government. If law is the promised word of the government, then fair enforcement is simply matching actions to words. Cárdenas had begun to learn of consistency—or rather, the lack of it—during Mr. Echverría's presidency. Now, Cárdenas was challenged by his own standards, and he tried to govern by them.

Cárdenas also brought experienced people into his administration, many with whom he had worked in other capacities and who had his trust and confidence. He saw that certain state officials of the previous administration were tried and sentenced for illegally selling state property such as cars for personal profit. This act was a statement against using public office for private gain, by now, the most serious problem pervading all of Mexico's politics.

At the same time, as city and municipal elections came around in the state, Cárdenas made it clear that open and honest elections would be honored. He picked no PRI candidate himself in the traditional party fashion. Anyone could run for municipal office.

There have always been small pockets of political independence and opposition, even in this popular governor's state. The National Action Party (PAN), representing mainly free market advocates and small business owners, won some mayoral races in Michoacán, and the state PRI-run government under Cárdenas honored those elections without trying to stuff ballot boxes or alter vote counts. This was another purposeful step toward cleaner government. Clean elections create an aura of true credibility around honestly elected leadership and help combat corruption because voters sincerely believe they can vote bad officials out of office.

Cárdenas assesses his term as governor as a positive one. The evidence would be the overwhelming state vote for him during the 1988 presidential race. Michoacán would become the bastion of the new *Cardenísmo* in the 1990s.

Although demands of state leadership kept Cárdenas busy, there was still time for family, or rather, like his father before him, Cuauhtémoc involved his family in his workaday political life. His wife, Celeste, shared his campaigning and the social responsibilities of a governor's wife, but family life was still her priority. During the governorship of Michoacán, their third child, a daughter, was born in 1983, and christened Camila. His sons, Lázaro and Cuauhtémoc, became trusted political aides, sharing day-to-day business of running the state government with their father.

While Cárdenas enjoyed success in state government, the national government had lost control of Mexico's economy. López Portillo had mortgaged practically all of the country's resources and industry to foreign lenders, financing senseless "modernization" while ignoring wasteful management. López Portillo himself employed several family member in useless government positions with huge bureaucratic salaries, fattening the family coffers. Then the world price of oil plummeted, and Mexico's debt almost doubled overnight. The peso was devalued from twenty-two per dollar to seventy per dollar. Suddenly, everything from tortillas to new cars cost more than three times what they had the week before.

Unchecked PRI authority throughout government had allowed gross negligence and rampant corruption. There was a growing comprehension among the common citizens in the street that this economic disaster did not have to happen. There were those in government responsible for this trouble, but with the reins of government and business and media in the tight grip of the few rich and powerful, what could be done?

López Portillo left the presidency in shame in 1982, and he had chosen a Harvard educated economist to succeed him, Miguel de la Madrid (1982-1988). De la Madrid was immediately forced to devalue the peso even more, to 150 to the dollar. All Mexicans suffered, but particularly the growing middle class that generally supports a nation's internal economy with its buying and selling of consumer and manufactured goods. Business fell into recession.

There was more voter turnout in 1982 than in any previous presidential election. The PAN following had clearly risen throughout the country, but once again, their opposition candidate was barely known. De la Madrid campaigned extensively, mouthing old promises of cleaner government. The voters responded to de la Madrid's calls for "a moral renovation of society," but his administration over the next six years would make little change.

He spoke up for "true representation" and for stronger, more independent legislature and court systems. He said he supported federalism, that is, the decentralizing of government. De la Madrid maintained that the "Party of Revolution" (PRI) was not in crisis, but halfway into his administration there was a growing number of radical opposition groups in southern Mexico. PAN was getting stronger in the north, and the mayoral offices in the huge cities of Juarez and Ciudad Chihuahua were conceded to PAN candidates. Even massive voter fraud couldn't keep these opposition wins from happening. In the gubernatorial races in the states of Nuevo León and Sonora, in 1985 PRI resorted to massive illegal voting to keep the offices in PRI control.

De la Madrid did manage to get inflation under control, and Mexico's debt was refinanced, but by late 1985 the national economy was almost frozen. Austerity measures were taken that left people unemployed. Poverty conditions even among the middle class were rising. Then, when it seemed things couldn't get worse, an earthquake struck central Mexico, nearly destroying the capital city and literally burying thousands of people.

The earthquake in September 1985 was the worst in the history of Mexico. Close to 50,000 lives were lost, most buried in the collapsed ruins of downtown Mexico

City. People poured into the streets to spontaneously organize rescue teams. Young people crawled into dangerous rubble, searching for survivors. The public called for international aid.

The government, with a detached pride and an unrealistic assessment of the crisis, announced that Mexico would accept no outside help, especially from the United States. Yet government resources and leadership were disorganized and slow in rescue and relief response. Instead of using the opportunity to prove its worth and ability, the government emergency efforts of rescue, survivor supply, and clean up planning were inadequate and chaotic. It has taken over a decade for the city to rebuild and regain normalcy.

The leadership of the Partido Revolucionario Institucional (PRI) had shown itself at its most inept and unresponsive during the crisis. The Mexican people were reaching the limits of their endurance and tolerance for "business as usual" in the ways Mexican government and business were being run. At this time when PRI leadership had a chance to be responsive to the needs and demands of the people, it failed.

The July 1986 race for governor of Chihuahua state produced a huge voter turnout in support of the PAN candidate. Voter surveys showed a 3-to-1 support of PAN, a vote of discontentment with PRI rather than a vote of support for the candidate himself. Yet PRI controlled the balloting sites and fraudulently claimed office. De la Madrid's "moral renovation" of the government was a sham.

There were massive street demonstrations throughout the state of Chihuahua and in other Mexican cities. PRI officials claimed that they were protecting the stable mechanisms of Mexican government from a conspiracy of the Catholic Church, the United States, and the small business class. Echoing voices of 1968, the government warned that public demonstration might be dealt with by force. More than ever before, there was a clear and growing gap between the needs and demands of the Mexican people and PRI leadership of the national government.

The political tensions in all of Mexico were heating toward a boil.

In the same year, 1986, Cuauhtémoc Cárdenas' term as governor of Michoacán came to an end. A new PRI bureaucrat was given the *dedazo* by de la Madrid, and he would win the governorship in classic PRI fashion. But Cárdenas was now more concerned with national policy being formulated. He had the respect and the attention of several major leaders of the party, and to them he began to articulate the idea of democratic change within the inner party.

CHAPTER VIII: The Democratic Current

In May of 1986, Cárdenas had met with Porfirio Muñoz Ledo, who had recently ended his term as Mexico's ambassador to the United Nations. The two men had a history of working together and sharing ideas, first meeting as young professionals in Paris, France, in 1957. They had worked together when Muñoz Ledo was Secretary of Labor during the Echeverría administration, and later, when he had been president of PRI while Cárdenas was governor of Michoacán.

Over a private meal in a Mexico City restaurant, they shared their concerns about Mexico's economic situation, the declining standard of living, and the way the government was abandoning old *Cardenísmo* ideals of managing the nation honestly for the benefit of the country's working people. By the end of the meal, they had decided to share these concerns with other old friends and political colleagues in the PRI, including Carlos Tello, Ifiginia Martínez, Leonel Durán, César Buenrostro, and others. All held important positions in the party and the government bureaucracy.

Together, these politicians began to formulate a policy statement to present to the rest of the PRI members. They felt that party policy needed to be reoriented economically. They felt that the party should comply with the letter and spirit of constitutional statutes in choosing and electing candidates to high office. They wanted to propose an internal party primary to select a party candidate for president, elected by all party members and not simply picked by the outgoing president.

This group agreed to meet again in July just as PRI was stealing the governorship from the National Action Party in Chihuahua. This time, even more party members attended the meeting, and they all began writing policy statement and discussing how to convince party leaders of the need for change. Although this gathering was intended as a quiet meeting to discuss new ideas, weeks later, a major national magazine announced that a small group of PRI party members, led by Cárdenas and Muñoz Ledo, had met to launch a new current of thought within the party. By August, the group was called the "Corriente Democrática," the Democratic Current.

To limit rumor and speculation, both Cárdenas and Muñoz read public statements trying to express the group's ideas. They called on the government to slow down the privatization of businesses, such as utilities and mining concerns, to pay off Mexico's debt. While some of the management of the economy had to come under more honest control, it was political change that was needed most, they argued. People wanted honestly elected officials, more choice, less corruption.

When Cárdenas' term as governor ended, he and other members of the Democratic Current were holding private discussions with President de la Madrid and PRI party president, Adolfo Lugo, about ways their group could express itself within the party structure. Privately, both PRI leaders agreed with the Democratic Current that change must occur, but they implied that "others" might not go along with such ideas of giving up personal power.

In their own private meetings, some Democratic Current members suggested that the group propose its own "sacrificial" candidate at the party's upcoming assembly to force the issue of choice with party conservatives. Some proposed Cárdenas for the role, and others proposed Mexico's ambassador to Spain, Rodolfo González Guevara. Still others proposed creating a document explicitly calling for a party primary while not suggesting any one particular candidate. They also continued meeting with de la Madrid and new PRI president, Hectór Luna de la Vega.

From these party leaders there were hints of political openings, and a reading of the Democratic Current's first working policy document was okayed by de la Madrid for the party assembly held in March of 1987. When Cuauhtémoc Cárdenas read this policy statement at a round table discussion, he was aggressively answered by PRI leader, de la Vega, and other party VIPs, denouncing the Democratic Current as a bunch of dissidents, destabilizers, and politically backwards troublemakers. The assembly ended under a cloud of uncertainty and division.

Cárdenas read a second policy statement a few days later in Michoacán before an applauding crowd of over 1,000 people, and weeks later a serious break with the Partido Revolucionario Institucional occurred. PRI officials removed from all party and government offices all signers of the Democratic Current document. Whether they renounced their party membership or were stripped of it, Democratic Current members were now out of the PRI party.

In early August 1987, President de la Madrid said that he would soon choose the next PRI candidate for president, announcing to all of Mexico that political life in Mexico would continue as always. Cuauhtémoc Cárdenas was a PRI outcast with few friends and only the strength of his convictions to stand on. His recent term as governor of Michoacán was being criticized and investigated for fraud now, too, by de la Madrid's chosen successor to that office, Luis Martínez Villicata. It was an attempt to distract the people and Cárdenas himself from the national political crisis. But the PRI would find no corruption in Cárdenas' previous administration in Michoacán to prosecute. Despite this negative propaganda, sixty-five percent of the state's voters would vindicate Cárdenas' term in office by voting for him as president in 1988.

During his ongoing debate with PRI leaders about a freer presidential election, Cuauhtémoc Cárdenas was informally approached by the leadership of other small, leftist political parties. They were feeling out Cárdenas' political stance. Cárdenas had long been a spokesman for traditional socialist policies, yet he was also considered a PRI insider, not completely trusted by the more radical and disaffected hard-line leftists. While these small parties had serious political differences, there were the first signs of a consensus growing among many people wanting change in Mexico's political system.

After de la Madrid's announcement that he would make the *dedazo* again, the governing director of the Federal District, Fernando Sánchez, announced a protest demonstration against "business as usual." He called for a "March of 100 Hours" in Mexico City as a pro-democracy show of support. The march was endorsed by Luis Sanchez Aguilar, the leader of the Popular Socialist Party (PPS– Partido Popular Socialista) and by other leftist political leaders. On September 19, 1987, from 5,000 to 8,000 people protested in the streets of the capital for 100 hours. Among them was Cuauhtémoc Cárdenas.

Nevertheless, in October, President de la Madrid made the *destape* that Carlos Salinas de Gotari would be the PRI's presidential candidate in 1988. Although a party outcast, Cárdenas was still formally a PRI party member. At this time, Cárdenas formally renounced his member- ship in the Partido Revolucionario Institucional, the great political machine that his own father had helped to found almost sixty years before.

Some time later, Carlos Cantú Rosas, the leader of the Authentic Party of the Mexican Revolution (PARM–Partido Aténtico de la Revolucíon Mexicana) asked Cuauhtémoc Cárdenas to be this party's official candidate for the pres- idency of Mexico. Most practical thinkers in Mexico at the time considered this a useless madness, trying to build a coalition of socialist, liberal sentiment. There was no money for campaigning. There was little political agree- ment among dozens of small parties that all despised the PRI's hold on power, but distrusted one another as well. Yet there was an underlying sense that people everywhere in the country wanted to take this fight for change to the PRI and its powerful lock on government control.

On November 29, 1987, Cuauhtémoc Cárdenas of- ficially announced his candidacy in Morelia in his home state of Michoacán, and the stage was set for the elec- tion of 1988 for the presidency of Mexico. Virtually no one predicted what was about to happen.

CHAPTER IX: Cárdenas and the Salinas Presidency

Although the Mexican people hoped for political change, no one could have predicted the results of the 1988 presidential election (see Chapter One) or the effects it would bring over the following weeks and during the six years of Carlos Salinas' presidency.

Officially, Salinas had been given 49.9% of the popular vote, Cárdenas 31.7%, and Manuel Clouthier, the PAN candidate, 16.9%, but no one believed these results. When the number of votes pouring in for Cárdenas had begun to alarm PRI election officials, the computerized tabulation process mysteriously collapsed. Later, the government explained that "the system had broken down." This official statement became a national joke of cynicism and contempt during the Salinas administration because the real breakdown had been in PRI's own image and in their management and control of the country.

Neither Manuel Clouthier nor Cuauhtémoc Cárdenas would officially acknowledge Salinas as the winner. The PAN organized a collection of 1.5 million signatures calling for a complete annulment of the election. Cárdenas called for a "national mobilization" of street protests throughout Mexico, but he did not endorse PAN's desire to anull the election, in part, because Cárdenas and his followers felt that they had actually won the election. He demanded an investigation of all voting results by independent judges via the constitutional process. But while PRI easily delayed the judicial process in the months to come, voting records would be "inadvertently destroyed" so the legitimacy of Salinas' election could never be proven one way or another.

Cuauhtémoc Cárdenas and his followers simply had no political clout to enforce his claims. In the early weeks after the 1988 presidential election, all of Mexico was in political turmoil. Cárdenas easily could have inflamed the country's political left, those parties that had joined together to support him and that had a historical reputation for agitation and violent confrontation. He could have stirred riot and perhaps even civil war in protest. But in the tradition of his father's style, Cárdenas chose not violent destruction of the system, but means to work for real change within Mexico's established political system. This peaceful stance helped to legitimize the country's leftist socialists groups as mature political participants within the process, to be seen less as mere destabilizers and radical anarchists.

Yet this huge political body within Mexico had no formal political instrument, no formal party or channel of communication with which to unite and effectively push for change. In 1989 Cárdenas and his advisors began to create a new, official political party in Mexico to confront PRI's monopoly on power.

A coalition of many small socialist, communist, and unionist parties had come together in the last few weeks before the 1988 election to endorse and support Cárdenas for president. He was formally the candidate of PARM, and his old engineering professor and friend of his father, Heberto Castillo, had declined the candidacy of the Mexican Socialist Party (PMS–Partido Mexciana Socialista) to back Cárdenas. Together, with members of the Democratic Current and other small parties, they formed the National Democratic Front (FDN–Partido Democrática Nacional). Its first national organization was for the 1988 election, and Cuauhtémoc Cárdenas was the national coordinator for it.

After the election, which the FDN felt had been stolen from their candidate, factions of this coalition vowed to unite as a formal political party. On May 5, 1989, the Revolutionary Democratic Party (PRD–Partido de la Revolucíon Democrática) was formally recognized by the federal government. This coalition was a merger of the Democratic Current and the Unified Socialist Party, the Workers Party, and other small, leftist groups. Cárdenas was elected president of the party at its first national congress, and he held the position through 1993. Immediately, PRD became the second largest and second most powerful political party in Mexico.

Under Cárdenas' leadership in its first years, the party

constantly confronted the Salinas administration, challenging the voting results in the November 1990 governor's race in the state of Tabasco. Salinas was forced to replace the PRI candidate, who had altered the vote count to win, with a more acceptable interim governor. In 1992, the governor-elect of Michoacán, Eduardo Villaseñor, was forced to renounce office because of disputed electoral procedures. Cárdenas' home state then became a bastion of new PRD political power and influence in Mexico.

The PRD proposed candidates and campaigned aggressively in many state elections after that. The party had 126 representatives in congress from 1989 through 1991 and only 41 deputy seats and four senate seats in the 1991-94 session due to the influence of negative propaganda by PRI. Yet Cárdenas' party fought on. Because of the 1988 election results and PRD's new political force, electoral reform began to take place. More representatives seats were added to both houses of congress, to be proportionally representative of the nation's population. The Federal Election Commission was overhauled, too, to insure cleaner, fairer elections in 1994.

The PRD and Cárdenas also campaigned against the new North American Free Trade Agreement (NAFTA) and Carlos Salinas' neoliberal economic policies. Neoliberalism was primarily the intensification of selling government-controlled businesses to private investors. While this measure did reduce foreign debt and spurred international investment, PRD argued that these policies only benefited the rich Mexican capitalist, not the common man in the street. The gap between rich and poor would continue to widen. Figures from Mexico's Institute of Statistics, Geography, and Information show that in the early 1990s, Mexico's richest 20% of the population was receiving 54% of the national wealth while the poorest 20% were getting only 5%. Yet internationally, Carlos Salinas was being considered the economic savior of Mexico. Cárdenas disagreed.

Cárdenas would stick to his socialist principles, which are the guiding foundation of his party. The PRD political platform calls for a new relationship between the national state and the people, economic development with social justice, and a democratic organization of government devoted to the law.

During Salinas' administration, Cárdenas and the PRD were subject to propaganda smears and even to violent repression by PRI supporters throughout the nation. In the final weeks of the 1988 campaign, Cárdenas' close friends and political advisors, Javier Ovando and Román Gil, were assassinated while sitting in a car in Mexico City. Cárdenas denounced this as a "message of intimidation" from the government itself. These men had worked for and supported Cárdenas and his beliefs since the 1970s. During Salinas' *sexenio*, 300 PRD party workers were killed in political confrontation nationwide as they worked for their beliefs and supported their candidates for office. The road to a more open democracy in Mexico had also become a bloody political battlefield.

By 1993 PRD was a political force to be reckoned with. Although PRI still held the reins of power, both PAN and PRD had formal representation in congress and in some state offices. Many state elections had been refuted and interim officeholders appointed as political opposition became more vocal and organized.

NAFTA became law in 1993, and Salinas' government, managed by mostly Harvard-educated economists, looked good on the world's accounting records. But employment and living conditions were still in a crisis stage for most Mexicans. Some election reform had been won, but PRI still manipulated elections and refused to recognize opposition victories. PRI still controlled politics and economics in Mexico, and they ran things according to old customs as much as they could. Yet Cuauhtémoc Cárdenas and his new political force had done much to effect change.

Late in 1993, Salinas gave his *destape* to Donaldo Colosio, a young and dynamic U.S.—educated economist, to be PRI's new presidential candidate. In response, PAN nominated Diego Fernández de Cevallos. Cuauhtémoc Cárdenas resigned as president of his party to become

PRD's first formal nominee for the presidency of Mexico. Once again, the political machinery of Mexico had been primed for a presidential election. And once again, no one in Mexico was ready for what would happen in 1994. Elections were becoming less and less business as usual.

CHAPTER X: The 1994 Election

The upcoming presidential election promised to be the cleanest, fairest election in Mexico's history. Cárdenas' previous showing and the rising political strength of PRD had forced concessions by PRI, including more equal access to the media and the presence of teams of independent, international observers to monitor the balloting process. Both Cevallos of PAN and Cuauhtémoc Cárdenas of PRD were gaining broader based support. Cárdenas was especially well-known now, not only for the name recognition of his father's past, but for his own political accomplishments.

But the PRI was confident. Salinas' (and the party's) neoliberal economic policies were being praised worldwide. Mexicans were optimistic about the future and were making positive international news. And PRI's candidate, Donaldo Colosio, was energetic and popular. He was promising many of the changes Cárdenas had campaigned for six years before, even if it made many of the old and powerful leaders or PRI—called "dinosaurs" by those advocating democratic change—uncomfortable.

Then on January 1, 1994, as the national campaign was beginning to shape up, Mayan peasants in the state of Chiapas rose in rebellion against Mexico's federal government. Calling themselves the Zapatista National Liberation Army (EZLN–Ejército Zapatista de Liberacíon Nacional), under the command of Subcommander Marcos, they took over several towns in the state, killing some soldiers. This Mayan peasant army was protesting the slave-like treatment of the native peoples by ruthless and government-supported rich landowners. This repression in Chiapas has been going on since colonial times. The Mayans demanded ownership rights to the long-exploited mountain land of their ancestors and the right to govern themselves. This act was a classic peasant revolt in the tradition of Emiliano Zapata's role in the Revolution of 1910. This was another outcry from Mexico's poorest people, announcing that despite appearances, Mexico had not changed. It was a more radical echo of what the new

Cardenísmo had been proclaiming for years now.

The Zapatista uprising in Chiapas frightened foreign investors and inflamed Mexican politics, dividing people passionately along economic lines. Poorer workers and peasants and social justice advocates tended to agree with and support the rebels. The richer classes called for army retaliation. International civil rights and humanitarian groups rushed to Chiapas, confounding the situation. Political tensions were rising in Mexico.

Then, only three months later, on March 23, Donaldo Colosio was assassinated in Tiajuana, Baja California, by a single gunman, shocking the nation. Many were afraid Mexico was on the brink of political chaos. Rumors and facts about the assassination, along with the Chiapas uprising, generated confusion and uncertainty. Campaign rhetoric fanned the flames of fear and crisis. Carlos Salinas was forced to reveal a new presidential candidate only six days later, naming Ernesto Zedillo, who had been Colosio's campaign manager, as the new PRI candidate.

Political uncertainty reigned in Mexico, and once again, Cuauhtémoc Cárdenas was in a position to affect the development of Mexico's modern political history. And again, the uncontrollable forces of PRI political power, the Mexican people's frame of mind, and Cárdenas' own personal campaign mistakes would conspire against him.

Ernesto Zedillo's personality was quite different from Colosio's—quiet, unassuming, and almost uncertain. And whose policies was he suddenly espousing—Colosio's, the PRI's, or his own? Like Colosio, Zedillo advocated electoral democratic change, but he also promoted the decades-long stability that PRI government had maintained in Mexico. This troubled year was no time for radical change in government, he proclaimed.

PAN's candidate, Cevallos, was a dynamic personality who represented conservative middle class business interest. He supported the economic promises of NAFTA and attracted younger voters who were more discontent with PRI rather than avidly for PAN political ideas. Cevallos is also a capable, articulate politician. In the first ever debate between presidential candidates in Mexico, which was another concession won by Cárdenas' new political strength, Cevallos clearly trounced the vague and uncertain Zedillo.

In the same debate, Cárdenas' own manner and style only damaged his image and influence. At heart, he is a quiet and shy person, often seeming reluctant to be cast in the public spotlight or politics. While he is an affectionate and good-humored family man and personal friend, he can be very formal and somber when speaking about political ideas and social justice, often grave to the point of ominous gloom. He doesn't have a sunny, smiling style of public contact that inspires attraction and comfort. He lacked a good media personality, relying on the gravity of substance rather than on slick appearance and style to win votes.

Despite advice from his campaign managers, Cárdenas mounted no showy campaign. He felt that he had won the 1988 election by sticking to his principles. He harangued against unemployment, the weakness of NAFTA and other economic problems, and the rise of crime. His own speeches, with their confrontational style and traditional socialist content and fiery rhetoric, tended to disturb voters rather than inspire confidence in his ability to lead the country. Post-election polls would later reveal that he wasn't really addressing the issues that were bothering most Mexicans in the year of upheaval, 1994.

Just weeks before the election, Cárdenas contributed to his own negative public appearance by meeting with Subcommander Marcos of the EZLN in Chiapas. New *Cardenísmo* still represents many aspects of his father's old *Cardenísmo*, especially land distribution to powerless peasants and social justice for the poorer classes, but the majority of Mexicans were uncomfortable with Marcos' more violent and radical communistic version of these same ideas. Their appearance together further served to disturb Mexican voters. Most Mexicans were not in the mood for more upheaval, and though many recognized the legitimacy of EZLN demands and of Cárdenas' claims of corruption and inefficiency in government, they wanted security and stability more.

In addition to Cárdenas' own campaigning style working against him, PRI still controlled the media. Television and radio covered staged events that attempted to link Cárdenas with fringe social groups like homosexuals and bizarre street people. Required to cover political parties other than PRI, media devoted more time to the PAN candidate when early polls showed strong Cárdenas support. Then they covered Cárdenas when Cevallos' popularity rose, trying to keep all PRI opposition support in conflict with itself. Post-election statistics would show Zedillo received over 40% of all television coverage. Cárdenas got around 8%, and Cevallos only 7% of the coverage. Radio coverage was even more slanted with 50% for Zedillo and the other 50% for all eight other candidates combined.

The vote on August 21, 1994, brought PRI candidate Zedillo to power with over 50% of the votes. Cevallos received 26.7%, and Cárdenas was third with only 16.7% of the vote. As much as Mexico's corrupt government troubled more people than ever before, they chose the known quantity of "business as usual" over more uncertain upheaval. Despite the promise of the 1988 election, and the clear and continuing need for democratic and economic change that he represented, despite his own personal integrity and his continued criticism of government corruption, Cuauhtémoc Cárdenas had hit a new low in political influence, clouding his future.

Adolfo Aguilar Zinzer, PRD member and Cárdenas' press secretary during the campaign, would later call for Cárdenas' retirement from public representation for the party. Zinzer felt that Cárdenas should become a silent, symbolic inspiration and leave real politics to younger PRD members. Cárdenas had failed to connect with Mexico's broad electorate, and because of party rules, he could not be reelected as his own party's president. It seemed his personal time on Mexico's political stage had come and gone. Despite changes he had forged in Mexico's democratic process and the cleanest election to date in the country's history, Cuauhtémoc Cárdenas' political influence was at a new low.

CHAPTER XI: Political Phoenix

Like the mythical bird that rose to new life from its own ashes, Cuauhtémoc Cárdenas' political life would revive in the following months, flying to a new level in 1997 never before achieved by an opposition politician in Mexico. The reasons for change would be a combination of his own ability to learn from his mistakes and the PRI's continued corruption and inability to change.

Just weeks after the election of Ernesto Zedillo (1994-2000) to Mexico's presidency, another political assassination occurred. This time it was Secretary General of PRI, José Ruiz Massieu, a powerful PRI insider and a former brother-in-law of outgoing President Salinas. In an attempt to stop public outcry before it could start, the government announced an immediate and independent investigation. But the investigation quickly pointed to conspiracy in the highest levels of PRI leadership, implicating even the respected Salinas family.

By December of 1994, Mexico was in political and economic chaos again. The *sexenio* of Carlos Salinas was revealed as an economic sham and the epitome of corruption for personal gain. Mexico's currency had to be suddenly devalued. Foreign investors pulled funds out of the country, and Mexico's stock market took a ten billion dollar plunge in value. Over the next weeks as Zedillo began his term, the loss would grow to 32 billion dollars. Stock value in Mexican corporations sustained a 70 billion dollar loss. Businesses would fail. Three million laborers would be laid off over the next twelve months. Mexico's entire economy faced massive bankruptcy.

The United States and the International Monetary Fund were called on to save Mexico from its sinking economic troubles. President Clinton, without congressional support, had to create a 20 billion dollar loan bailout to help Mexico's economy. Through NAFTA and other social factors, the two countries have become so economically linked that, for the best or the worst, one nation's situation is irrevocably affected by the other, culturally, politically, and economically.

As 1995 dawned, Mexico was in its worst political and economic crisis ever. The peso went through another 35% devaluation. Wages and prices were frozen. Massive unemployment occurred. Crime rose. Police corruption nationwide was further exposed, especially in connection to drug trafficking into the United States. The Salinas family was scandalized in connection to this situation, and many feared that Mexico was becoming a narco-democracy like Columbia, terrorized by cartel drug money and armed power. Public anger was rising. By the end of 1995, polls would show that 87% of Mexico's people had "little or no trust" in government. In 1996, the "progressive decadence" in Mexico, as some writers labeled it, continued to grow.

In his inaugural speech in December, 1994, President-elect Zedillo had been forced to publicly concede the need for PRI leadership to face a new reality in Mexico. He admitted the need for, and promised, new political party funding rules, fair and equal media access for all candidates, and more autonomy of election authorities. He promised to give up the *dedazo*, the tradition of the president hand-picking his successor. He announced a new Campaign Against Corruption, and stated specifically that government was not a place to amass personal wealth.

There would also be new electoral concessions, Zedillo promised. One of these would be the democratic election, for the first time ever, of the mayor of Mexico City. Some consider this office the second most powerful position in Mexico's political structure. Previously, the president had always chosen a man to fill the position. Once again, the political fortunes of Cuauhtémoc Cárdenas would rise in the fires of new political change in Mexico.

Late in 1996, Cárdenas became PRD's first candidate for the mayorship of Mexico City. He knew the people were in the mood for change, but he also knew that he must learn from the 1994 election and offer not only good policy, but also the image of leadership that voters were comfortable with. Cárdenas knew he must appeal to a broader based public, the moderate and middle class, not just to the interests of the socialist left.

He moved closer to the center of Mexico's political spectrum by accepting NAFTA, saying it could be altered to further help the lowest economic classes. He acknowledged the necessities of capitalism, arguing only that neoliberalism should have a more social orientation, helping those who need it the most. Cárdenas' speeches became less confrontational in tone, guaranteeing political stability and the interests of capitalism, but he still was demanding more democratic choice, social reform, and better economic conditions for the working classes.

Heeding the recommendations of advisers, Cárdenas' campaign style also changed as he tried to appear less wooden and somber, smiling more, keeping his messages to the city's people upbeat and optimistic. He still carried the aura of his father's mystique, but in the age of instant mass media, his own demeanor and ideas, more than family history, had to inspire trust and confidence in the voters.

While PRI's popularity with the public had diminished, the party was still the power of the nation, and it nominated Alfredo del Maza as its mayoral candidate. PAN's popularity as a political party had also grown, its candidate having come in a strong second in the 1994 presidential election. Their mayoral candidate in 1997 was Carlos Castillo Peraza. In challenge to these parties, Cárdenas' PRD had to raise its public image and clearly define its ideological differences with the other parties.

If elected, Cárdenas assured the city's public employees that no honest workers would be fired just because they were PRI members. He also promised to promote small business to help create jobs and to promote private investment in public works. He also promised government housing assistance to the capital's poorest inhabitants.

His major promise was to fight crime in the city. Due to Mexico's economic depression, unemployment was bad, and may desperate people were forced to crime for survival. From the 1960s to 1994, Mexico City's crime rate doubled. It doubled again from 1994 to 1997, in just three short years.

Mexico City is arguably the world's largest city, a mega–metropolis with mega–social and mega–economic problems. There are 19 million people in the metro area and perhaps 30 million in the entire Federal District. One quarter of Mexico's annual Gross National Production is generated in the city as is three quarters of the nation's business action. The traffic and pollution are a nightmare. The city's poorest barrios (neighborhoods) are virtual camps of cardboard and tin houses with no electrical or sanitation services. The gap between rich and poor grows daily, and given Mexico's shattered economy and unemployment, crime in Mexico City is its most feared and complex problem. Whoever presides over Mexico City's government inherits by election some of the world's most difficult urban problems.

On July 6, 1997, Cuauhtémoc Cárdenas was voted in as Mexico City's first freely elected mayor with over 47% of the votes. It was Mexico's cleanest election in history, a victory, Cárdenas declared, for parliamentary democracy. The PRI candidate received only 25% of the vote, and the PAN candidate around 16%. Cuauhtémoc Cárdenas had just won the right to deal with Mexico's largest social and economic problems. President Ernesto Zedillo publicly congratulated Cárdenas on his victory and congratulated Mexico on its new "democratic fiesta".

The election was a triumph for the Party of the Democratic Revolution. On the wave of Cárdenas' popularity, the PRD swept many candidates into office during this off-year election. For the first time ever, PRI lost its majority rule in the legislative assembly. Nationwide, PRD also now controlled six of the 31 governorships. Democratic change had truly begun to appear in Mexico's modern political history, and its primary driving force has been Cuauhtémoc Cárdenas.

CHAPTER XII: Cárdenas & Mexico in the 21st Century

With the birth of a new democratic order in Mexico, the nation's political life has improved. Mexico today is a more open society. There is more independent freedom of the press and public debate between candidates. In 1999 the PRI held its first inner-party primary to choose its next presidential candidate as Ernesto Zedillo announced the end of the presidential *dedazo*. Cárdenas had been calling for this action since 1986. More opposition party members than ever before now hold important government positions, including the Attorney General's office. They have more representation and political power in congress. But the changes have come only from hard political work and sacrifice. From 1989 to 1997, over 500 PRD election workers lost their lives fighting for political voice in Mexico.

While Mexico's democratic health is better, economic and urban woes still abound. Many of Cárdenas' political opponents were happy to saddle him with the city's unsolvable modern problems. And since assuming office in December 1997, Cárdenas' political effectiveness and his popularity have suffered as he has faced the day-to-day reality of running a city. The problems that go with trying to govern the world's largest city have given his adversaries ammunition for their political attacks.

Many claim that Cárdenas has failed to "take back the city" from criminals and crime gangs. In 1998, Cárdenas was forced to fire his chief of police, a retired army colonel, because of scandalous allegations by all three major political parties. While Cárdenas claims that statistics show reductions in car theft, bank robberies, and death rates related to crime, the average citizen of Mexico City, living within the daily urban chaos, maintains the sense that crime and living conditions have worsened.

Cárdenas' administration also claims improvements in public health programs such as family planning, child nutrition education, and drug and alcohol rehabilitation. Clean water production has been increased, and street lighting and paving have improved parts of the city. More money has been pumped into public education and into ecological clean-up. Commercial centers have been created, but attempts to relocate street venders there have been controversial.

While changes in Mexico's government have allowed more public scrutiny than ever before, the irony is that criticism of Cárdenas has mounted. Many argue that Cárdenas has little to show for the big expectations that followed his election. Yet even the Mexico City head of PAN, Gonzalo Altamirano, has stated that Cárdenas has made "an effort worthy of consideration to fight corruption at any cost." And no one person will ever solve all the vast urban and economic problems of Mexico City.

While his administration has been criticized, as are all administrations in democratic countries, Cuauhtémoc Cárdenas' personal integrity, his reputation for honorable commitment to honest, clean government remains in tact. He is still the spiritual leader as well as the most influential spokesman for Mexico's modern socialist policies, especially for the Party of the Democratic Revolution, now Mexico's second most powerful political party. He still advocates policy that involves and betters the lives of Mexico's poorest citizens.

Acting in this capacity, Cárdenas decided in May 1999 to accept the nomination of the Labor Party as its presidential candidate in 2000. He cited his purpose as being "to consolidate a grand coalition of democratic organizations, which will be the base of the republic's next government." A few months later, he also accepted the nomination of his own party, PRD. Cuauhtémoc Cárdenas' third try for the presidency was in full and formal gear.

Prior to these nominations, Cárdenas sought to create The Grand Opposition Alliance (Gran Alianza Opositara) to establish an ultimate democratically chosen candidate to face and defeat the PRI candidate in 2000. The coalition would have policy points that all citizens believe in: more democracy, more economic development for the poor, justice and due process of law for all, and defense of national sovereignty. Cárdenas proposed that issues dividing the individual parties such as the management of petroleum reserves, the privatizing of electrical utilities, the cost of higher education, and how to resolve the conflict in Chiapas, should be put to a vote within the coalition.

Cárdenas proposed a unification across Mexico's political spectrum, including PAN's conservative members. But his acceptance of a presidential nomination by a coalition of leftist parties, which included the Workers Party, the Social Alliance Party, the Labor Party, and PRD, served to define political differences in Mexico today. In the spring of 1999 PAN nominated its own presidential candidate, Vincente Fox, a well-known business leader. The PRI held its first ever inner-party primary that summer, choosing Zedillo's Minister of the Interior, Francisco LaBastida Ochoa, as their candidate. LaBastida is a 37-year old career politician who is promising yet more gradual reform of Mexico's political process. Mexico's presidential election of 2000 would shape up to be a three-man race in an honestly contested democratic process.

The presidential election of July 2, 2000, was won by PAN candidate Vincente Fox, ushering in a new era for Mexican democracy. With a majority of the popular vote, Fox was victorious over PRI candidate Francisco Labastida Ochoa and Cuauhtémoc Cárdenas of the PRD. Cárdenas also represented the Alianza por Mexico, comprised of the Workers Party (PT), the Socialist Alliance Party (PAS), the Convergence for Democracy, and the Nationalist Society Party (PSD), along with PRD. Part of the nation's leftist popular vote went to Porfirio Muñoz Ledo, Cárdenas' past political ally, who represented PARM.

Much analysis of this dramatic change in Mexico's political history will be written in the coming years, including explanations of why Cárdenas lost his third bid for his nation's presidency. Whatever the conjecture and opinion of Cárdenas' political role, past, present, and future; whatever the success or failure of Vincente Fox's presidency; Mexico's new democracy is flourishing, and it is rooted in the convictions, actions, and personal history of Cuauhtémoc Cárdenas, one of Mexico's finest political statesmen.

GLOSSARY OF TERMS

Caudillo—Regional military leader with an army not necessarily loyal to the nation; during and after the Mexican Revolution of 1910, many caudillos governed regions of Mexico as unofficial dictators who traded armed might for political and economic concessions from the federal government.

Communism—This political theory advocates the principles of socialism, but with an emphasis on violent revolutionary struggle in which the working classes take control of a nation's government and resources. (See socialism.)

Constitution of 1917—Largely based on the constitution of the United States, two of its articles have been the cause of much political conflict in Mexico; Article 27 makes private ownership of property subordinate to public or national interests, with government ownership of all subsoil rights; Article 123 protects the rights of industrial and agrarian laborers, recognizing the right to organize and strike to improve conditions, the right to an 8–hour work day and a minimum wage.

Destape—A Spanish word meaning "revelation"; a term that describes the Mexican president's choice of a party candidate to succeed him.

Dedazo—A Spanish word meaning "the big finger"; the term refers to the Mexican president's pointing out who will be his choice of political party friends to succeed him as president.

Ejido—When Mexico's government distributed land to peasants, the federal government retained ownership of the land but put huge tracts of land under the cooperative management of village and community committees, called ejidos, which in turn distributed the land to local individuals to use as they pleased.

Federalism—Advocates the decentralizing of federal government, a separation of branches of government and a system of checks and balances; it can also mean a return to local power authority or caudillo rule.

NAFTA—The North American Free Trade Agreement (NAFTA) established a free trade zone among Mexico,

Canada and the United States. By eliminating customs duties on trade between Mexico and the United States, it allowed many businesses to establish manufacturing plants in Mexico. It also allowed many American companies to export food and other products to Mexico duty free.

Neoliberalism—Also known as "social liberalism" this refers to President Salinas' support of laissez faire business, or unhampered free trade; this meant support of NAFTA, the export of raw materials and the import of foreign-made goods and foreign investment capital; it also advocated the privatization of businesses controlled by the Mexican government by selling them to private business concerns.

Sexenio—A term that refers to the Mexican president's six-year term in office.

Socialism—A principal political theory advocating the collective (or government) ownership and management of a nation's production and the distribution of goods and services; advocates cooperation and social service for all people, as opposed to the scarcity, competition, and profit basis of capitalism.

Spoils system—When newly elected politicians fill government job openings and award business contracts or other favors to friends and relatives; when these politicians are defeated in office, their replacements repeat the process with their own supporters, friends, and families.

POLITICAL PARTY ACRONYMS

There are many political parties in Mexico and they are most often referred to by abbreviated name or acronym. Below is a list of the major parties listed by their acronym:

PAN—Partido Accíon Nacional, or the National Action Party, formed in 1938, is composed mostly of small business owners and conservative Catholics, and is Mexico's oldest opposition party. It favors less government intervention in the national economy, is free market oriented, and wants more state and municipal independence from the national government.

PARM—Partido Auténtico de la Revolucíon Mexicano, or the Authentic Party of the Mexican Revolution, was formed by old revolutionaries and small-time caudillos, and considered conservative and generally against agrarian reform.

PPS—Partido Popular Socialista, or the Socialist People's Party, espouses radical socialist policy.

PRD—Partido Revolucionario Democrática, or Party of the Democratic Revolution, is the party formed in 1989 by Cárdenas and members of the Democratic Current, the Unified Socialist Party, the Workers Party, and other small, leftist groups. It is currently the second most powerful political party in Mexico.

PRI—Partido Revolucionario Institucional, or the Institutional Revolutionary Party, is the strongest political party in Mexico, in power so long, it is virtually indistinguishable from the government itself. It is a kind of closed bureaucratic club that strives to maintain control of the government, using it as a means to amass personal business wealth. At present, its policies advocate neoliberalism, favor NAFTA and free market trade, and privatization of businesses controlled by the national government.

PRM—Partido Revolucionario Mexicano, or the Mexican Revolutionary Party. It is the second name of the PRI party.

PRN—Partido Revolucionario Nacional, or the National Revolutionary Party, the first name of the PRI party, formed by President Elías Calles in 1928, and consolidated by President Lázaro Cárdenas. This party brought together all the powerful political interests in Mexico to govern by jointly choosing a president and ruling by consensus.

PT—Partido del Trabajo, or the Workers Party, espouses more radical socialist policies.

TO LEARN MORE

These books about Mexico were all written by American journalists who are specialists on Latin American affairs. While they are intended for adult readers, all three are written in a modern style accessible and interesting to most young people.

Bordering On Chaos: Mexico's Roller-Coaster Journey Toward Prosperity, By Andres Oppenheimer. Little, Brown, and Company, 1996.

Mexico: Biography of Power (A History of Modern Mexico 1810-1996), by Enrique Krause. HarperCollins Publishers, 1997.

Distant Neighbors: A Portrait of the Mexicans, by Alan Riding. Vintage Books, 1986.

Sources on the Internet:

Web Sites:

<www.cen-prd.org.mx> Homepage for Partido Revolcionario Democrática

<www.pan.org.mx> Homepage for Partido Acción Nacional

<www.pri.org.mx> Homepage for Partido Revolucionario Institucional

(These web sites are all in Spanish and without English translation.)

<www.agora.stm.it/elections> This web site is Wilfried Dirksen's Elections Around the World. It is in English and has links to information on recent elections in many countries, including Mexico. It also contains statistical information and links to many of Mexico's political parties' web sites.

Index

The Contemporary Profiles and Social Policy Series for the Younger Reader features biographies of prominent national and international persons. Other individuals that have been included in this series are Henry B. Gonzalez, Nancy Landon Kassebaum, Rigoberta Menchú Túm, Mary Robinson, and Father Roy Bourgeois.